I Love
CONSTRUCTION
VEHICLES

Silver Dolphin

Silver Dolphin Books
An imprint of Printers Row Publishing Group
10350 Barnes Canyon Road, Suite 100, San Diego, CA 92121
www.silverdolphinbooks.com

Printers Row Publishing Group is a division of Readerlink Distribution Services, LLC.

The Silver Dolphin Books name and logo are trademarks of Readerlink Distribution Services, LLC.

All notations of errors or omissions should be addressed to Silver Dolphin Books, Editorial Department, at the above address.
All other correspondence (author inquiries, permissions) concerning the content of this book should be addressed to
Quarto Children's Books, The Old Brewery, 6 Blundell Street, London N7 9BH

This book was designed and produced by
QUARTO CHILDREN'S BOOKS

Author Chris Oxlade
Designer Andrew Crowson
Paper Engineer Jayne Evans
Model illustration Andrew Crowson
Editor Suhel Ahmed
Managing Editor Diane Pengelly
Creative Director Jonathan Gilbert
Publisher Zeta Jones

ISBN: 978-1-62686-562-4

Manufactured, printed, and assembled in China

19 18 17 16 15 1 2 3 4 5

CONTENTS

CONSTRUCTION VEHICLES

Giant machines do many jobs at **construction sites**, **quarries**, and **mines**. Huge diggers scoop up soil from the ground. Monstrous dump trucks rumble along as they carry heavy loads. Other machines push soil and **rubble** around, lift building materials, and dig underground.

Arm

Diggers don't just dig holes in the ground. They lift and carry heavy things from place to place, and also load soil and rubble into trucks.

Bucket

Dump trucks have huge wheels. They carry rock and rubble from one place to another. They're too big to drive on normal roads.

Powerful engine

If you need to push around piles of soil, sand, rock, or rubble, you need a powerful bulldozer with a big blade at the front.

Bucket-wheel excavators are enormous machines that work in quarries and mines. They dig out huge loads of rock or coal.

DIGGERS

Diggers, also called excavators, scoop earth out of the ground with a bucket on the end of an arm. They move along on caterpillar tracks, which are chains of metal plates around the wheels. The tracks keep the heavy machine from sinking into soft ground.

A digger's jointed arm is a bit like a human arm. It has a shoulder joint, an elbow joint, and a wrist joint. The bucket can reach deep into the ground or be lifted high in the air.

The joints on a digger's arm are moved by rams. Each ram is fitted to a steel tube that is pushed in and out of a cylinder. This is called a piston.

Shoulder joint

Metal plates

Caterpillar tracks are made of metal plates that are linked together to make a loop. The tracks go around the wheels.

Elbow joint

Wrist joint

Bucket teeth

The driver controls the digger's arm from inside a cab. He has foot pedals to make the caterpillar tracks roll forward or backward.

LOADERS

The name of this machine gives a huge clue about the job it does. It loads stuff into trucks. The loader scoops up soil or rubble from the ground, lifts it high into the air, drives it to a truck, and drops it in.

Metal bucket

The driver inside the cab uses levers to lower the bucket to the ground, and then drives the loader into a pile of soil or rubble. The teeth on the end of the bucket can push it deep into the pile.

A loader's bucket is connected to two strong arms. These lift the bucket into the air.

Wh[ee]l [lo]aders have [four w]heels
[with big] tires [and] a dies[el engine ...]ab.

Driver's cab

[...]er arms

[...]der is used
[when] there's
only a small pile of
rubble to m[ove ...]e
[...]
loade[r ...]

DIGGING TOOLS

Diggers are fitted with a variety of tools so they can do different jobs. The tools include smaller buckets, augers, and breakers. On some diggers, the bucket at the end of its arm can be replaced by a different tool.

A narrow, toothed bucket is used to dig deep trenches in the ground. These trenches are filled with **concrete** to make **building foundations**, or pipes are laid down to make drains.

Narrow bucket

A wide bucket is used for scooping up big loads of soil or... ...th ca... the ...

A breaker is a noisy drill that f... on a digger's arm. The drill has a sharp p... called a drill bit, to smash concrete ... by bashing it again and again.

An auger is a giant screw used to dig deep holes. As it turns, the au... pushes into the ground and lift... earth to the top of the screw...

Drill bit

DUMP TRUCKS

Dump trucks (sometimes called dumper trucks) carry rocks, sand, and rubble around construction sites, quarries, and mines. They have chunky tires to drive over soft ground and along uneven roads.

Dump trucks have
carrying space
back called a
It is design
carry hea

Chunky tires

An average dump truck can carry 40 tons of material. That's about the same as the weight of six African elephants.

Powerful rams push the front end of the cargo bed up. This makes the load slide out onto the ground.

Tipping cargo bed

A tipper truck is designed to drive on roads rather than on rough construction sites. Tippers deliver gravel, sand, and other materials to the site.

GIANT DUMP TRUCKS

The dump trucks that work in quarries and mines are gigantic. They carry rock or coal from where it is dug out to the place where it is stored and processed. The biggest trucks can carry an amazing 400 tons of rock.

Giant dump trucks are so large that the driver has to climb up a long ladder to reach the driver's cab high above the ground.

Roof protects cab

Ladder

The wheels and tires of giant dump trucks are taller than an adult human being.

The machines that load big dump trucks are just as massive as the trucks themselves. The... bucketfuls... dump tru...

A dump truck drives its load t... ers... needed... up the load are driven by **hydraulic** power.

Ram...

Tipping load

BULLDOZERS

With a huge blade at the front and giant caterpillar tracks at the sides, a bulldozer is designed to shove piles of soil ~~e, and ston~~ ~~hty~~ engine drives the track ~~ers~~ are slo~~ but ~~owerful.

~~lic rams~~

A b~~
and~~
blade. ~~lic~~ rams lift the blade up and lower it ~~he~~ ground.

Wide tracks give the bulldozer lots of grip in soft ground. Unlike tires, tracks will not get stuck in soft ground.

Metal plates

Most bulldozers have fierce-looking claws at the back. These are used for breaking up hard ground.

Claws

Bulldozers are designed to work on uneven ground. They can also drive up and down steep slopes.

OTHER EARTH MOVERS

These heavy machines not only spread out sand and gravel, but they also flatten the earth to make the ground hard and level. Road-building companies use them to prepare the ground before laying **asphalt**.

This is a self-propelled scraper. It has a sharp blade underneath that scrapes off a layer of earth as it moves along.

Towed scraper

Blade

This is a towed scraper, which doesn't have its own engine. A tractor pulls it along to flatten the ground.

Bulldozing blade

This machine is called a grader. It is a cross between a bulldozer and a scraper. It spreads sand and gravel evenly to make the ground smooth and flat.

Toothed wheels

Rollers are machines with heavy, toothed wheels. The wheels flatten the ground. This roller is called a compaction roller.

145

DO NOT PUSH

MOBILE CRANES

A mobile crane is a truck with a lifting arm called a crane mounted on top. Mobile cranes visit construction sites to lift and move concrete and heavy pieces of steel called girders. The tallest mobile cranes are more than 300 feet high.

Boom section

A mobile crane has a special arm called a telescopic boom. It is made of sections that slide out from each other to make the boom longer.

Steel girder

XCMG QY100K

Operator's cab

Driver's cab

This twelve-wheeler mobile crane has two cabs, one for driving along the road, and one for operating the crane.

Before putting a crane's boom up, the operator pulls out the crane's feet from all four sides. The feet keep the crane from toppling over.

Pulley wheels

Crane's foot

A big lifting hook dangles from the end of the boom. The hook is connected to the boom by metal wires that go around pulley wheels.

Lifting hook

TOWER CRANES

Tower cranes help people make very tall buildings. They lift construction materials high up in the air to where they are needed. A tower crane has a long, thin boom on top that can turn a full circle.

Boom

Support rods

The height of tower cranes can be changed. To make the crane taller, the top of the tower is lifted. Then the new section of tower is added at ground level, and slotted into place.

Hook

To keep the tower crane from toppling over, a heavy **counterweight** is added to the back of the long boom.

A tower crane operator can't be afraid of heights! The operator's cab is at the top of the tower and spins around with the boom.

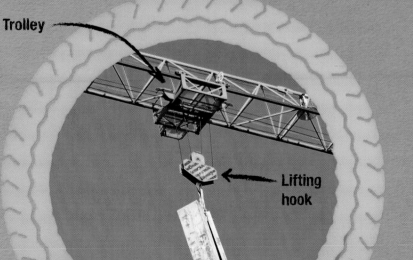

Counterweight

Trolley

The lifting hook hangs from a trolley that the operator moves backward and forward along the boom.

Lifting hook

CONCRETE MIXERS

A concrete mixer is a special truck for mixing concrete and taking it to the construction site. It has a drum that mixes the concrete. The drum turns, or rotates, stirring the concrete inside. It can even turn while the truck is on the move.

A motor turns the rotating drum. When the drum turns, large blades (called vanes) on the inside of the drum lift and mix the concrete.

Rotating drum

Concrete mixers are filled at concrete plants, either with ready-mixed concrete or the materials to make concrete (cement, sand, gravel, and water).

When the drum turns in the other direction, the concrete comes pouring out. It slides down a delivery chute.

Delivery chute

A concrete pump pushes wet concrete up through a pipe to the upper floors of a building. The pump is driven by a motor.

MINE MONSTERS

This digging machine, called a bucket-wheel excavator, is used at **opencast mines** and quarries. The main part of the machine is the wheel itself, which has huge buckets around its rim. As the wheel turns, the buckets reach into the ground and scoop up great chunks of rock or coal.

Supporting wires

The bucket wheel dumps rock or coal onto the top of the arm. The arm has a moving strip called a conveyor belt that takes the load to a collection point.

Bucket wheel

Bucket excavators move around on giant tracks, but very slowly!

Teeth

Each bucket on the giant wheel is as big as the bucket on a construction digger (see page 6). The sharp teeth cut into the hard ground.

Giant loaders also work at mines and quarries. They scoop up loose coal or rock and load it into dump trucks.

TUNNELING MACHINES

Tunneling machines work under the ground. These amazing machines cut away rock as they burrow through the earth, like a giant worm. They get rid of waste material, and also build a lining inside the new tunnel.

Cutter head

There is a huge rotating cutter head on the front end of a tunneling machine. The cutter head has many sharp teeth that slice and grind away at the rock as it turns.

A solid round section known as a cylinder is fixed behind the cutting head. It prevents the new tunnel from collapsing.

Cylinder

As the tunneling machine moves forward through the rock, concrete pieces are put around the new tunnel to support its walls, and to keep water out.

To start making a new tunnel, a tunneling machine is carefully lowered down a **shaft** to the place where it will start to dig.

MODEL ASSEMBLY INSTRUCTIONS

Place the bottom edges of the box and lid together to form your scene, and then build the models. Press out the model pieces and separate into four piles for the A, B, C, and D pieces. All the pieces are numbered to help you match them up: slot 1 to 1, 2 to 2, and so on.

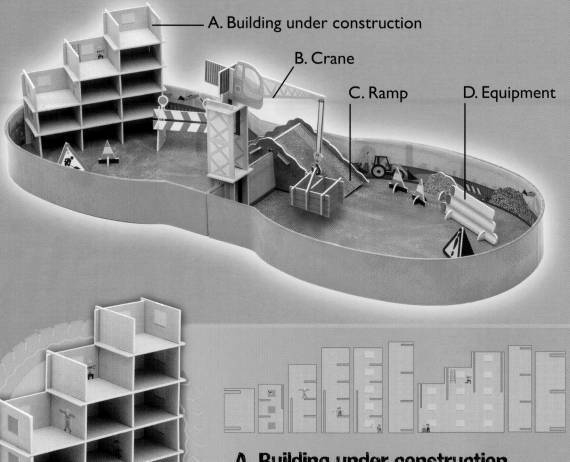

A. Building under construction

B. Crane

C. Ramp

D. Equipment

A. Building under construction

Slot together the side walls to the back piece so that the blue windows are on the inside. Then slot in the floors, from the base to the top.

B. Crane

Build the tower, then assemble the boom and place it on top. Slot the section into the center of the scene, where the edges of the box and lid meet. Build the crate and hang it on the hook.

C. Ramp

Line up the triangular side pieces and then slot in the two top pieces. Slot the ramp into the central edges of the box next to the crane.

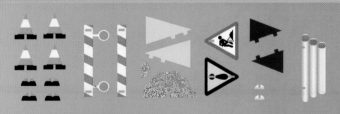

D. Equipment

Slot the correct base pieces and stands to the equipment by matching up the numbers. Finally, place them in the scene.

GLOSSARY

asphalt A dark material that roads are covered in to give them a smooth, flat finish.

building foundation A stone or concrete structure that supports the building from underneath.

cargo bed The boxlike space at the back of a truck for carrying the load.

concrete A hard, strong construction material used to build walls and floors.

construction site The area in which a building is being made. For safety reasons, only workers are allowed in this area.

counterweight A weight that is added to one end of a construction vehicle to keep it from toppling over.

hydraulic Mechanical movement that is powered by water.

mine An underground pit or tunnel from which minerals (like coal) are taken.

opencast mine A pit above the ground from which minerals (like coal) are taken.

quarry An open area that is dug up for materials such as stone, slate, and limestone.

rubble Broken pieces of stone and brick that have fallen from old walls or buildings when they were knocked down.

shaft A passageway used to send machines (like a tunneling machine) and workers down to a mine.